Dear Parents:

Ready Reader Storybooks™ have been developed with your kinder-
garten through second-grader in mind. This series is designed to
encourage young readers to begin to read alone, thus increasing basic
reading skills. The simple stories have easy-to-follow plots, and the
bright, colorful illustrations add to the fun, and provide the visual
appeal that helps to promote and enhance your youngster's reading
experience.

The stories in this series vary in subject matter and style, so your
child will be sure to find stories of interest. The large type is easy to
read, and the format is just the right size for small hands to hold.
The Ready Reader Storybooks™ will delight while developing and
encouraging your child's independent reading skills.

Duffy Takes a Dip

Written by Jean Davis Callaghan
Illustrated by Joan Thoubboron

Modern Publishing
A Division of Unisystems, Inc.
New York, New York 10022

"Good morning, Mama and Papa," the seven ducklings say.

"Good morning, ducklings."

"Today I will teach you how to swim," says Mama.
"Come, follow me."

Duffy would rather play on the shore.

"Come along, Duffy," says Mama.

"Try to do what I do," Mama tells the ducklings.

All the ducklings try—except Duffy.

His brothers and sisters call,
"Look, Duffy!"

"Can you do this, Duffy?" they ask.

"Come on, Duffy, swim with us!"

"One, two, three, four, five, six ducklings," Papa counts. "Where's Duffy?"

Papa finds Duffy hiding on
the shore.
"I'm afraid of the water,"
Duffy says.

"When I was young, I was afraid of the water, too," Papa tells him.

Papa takes Duffy for a ride on his back.

"Oh, this is fun!" says Duffy.

"Look at the fish, Papa!"

"The water feels good!"
Duffy says.

"And it's fun to splash!"

"Papa," Duffy laughs, "I can see myself!"

Soon Duffy is swimming all by himself. "Weeeee!"